What if there was more to life…?

A guide to help you restore the power Allah has gifted you with, to live life with a content heart and a lucid mind

MAARIA DEEM

This is a work of a non-fiction, self-help, book.

Copyright © 2022 Maaria Deem

All rights reserved. No parts of this book may be reproduced or used in any manner without written permission of the copyright owner except for the use of quotations in the book review.

To request permission contact: Maariadeem@gmail.com

Edited by: Mr. Abdul Quddoos Ahmad

Printed independently through KDP

Author's website: www.maariadeem.com

First paperback edition September 2022

For my mum who taught me how to walk,

For my dad who showed me the destination,

For my brother & my two sisters for always giving me a reason to get back up again every time I fell.

And lastly, for my uncle Abdul Quddoos, who selflessly helped me bring this book to you.

Thank you.

Content table

Part one

Introduction... 1

The hidden power.. 4

After darkness comes light 6

The power of thought... 13

Hidden gifts.. 22

The three Q's.. 27

Part two

Believe in your power

Your existence is far more powerful than you comprehend......................... 31

The first step.. 31

Nothing is too much for Him.. 32

When challenges arise... 32

Through the bad... 33

Don't stop shining, my friend... 33

Don't stop praying.. 34

Focus on the journey not the destination.. 34

Believe me, it all works out in the end... 34

You are more than what they think of you as.. 35

The best is yet to come.. 36

Part three

The key... 37

Gems from the Quran... 42

Virtues of sending peace and blessings upon the prophet SAW................. 45

Part four

Use you power………………………………………………………………………....…..47

CONGRATULATIONS……………………………………………………………..……………….92

Introduction

Discover your power

$$\text{(قُلْ إِنَّمَا أَنَا بَشَرٌ مِّثْلُكُمْ)}$$

Indeed, I am a human just like you

(Al Kahaf: 110)

The words that Rasool Allah ﷺ would constantly use to remind us that he, in nature is no different from us.

Just like you and I, he ﷺ would feel hungry if he hadn't eaten in a while. He would feel tired if his blessed body needed sleep, and he would feel hot if the sun shone too bright.

Just like you and I, he ﷺ experienced all kinds of emotions, from happiness, excitement, and relief to sorrow, pain and fear.

And that my friend, is the greatest evidence that the problem doesn't lie in the way we feel. The problem doesn't lie in the sadness you bear, or the worries you experience. Neither does it lie in feeling low when you're expected to be over the moon, or in being charged with excitement over the very things those around you perceive as insignificant.

The problem was never about how you feel, it was never about **controlling** your emotions because they never appeared for you to control in the first place. Additionally, the problem **doesn't** lie in the situations you face either, whether that's losing your job or falling out with someone close. The problem doesn't lie in misplacing your car keys or being betrayed by someone you trusted.

In essence, the key is being able to **navigate** through every challenge with an Allah-conscious mind that expects only the best and sees only the best and finds only the best, and hence receives only the best from the owner of all the best.

It has been mentioned in a prophetic saying, that Allah ﷻ says:

أنا عند ظنّ عَبدي بي

I am what my servant thinks of me

(Bukhari and Muslim)

My and your Allah is the same Allah that split the ocean for Mousa عليه السلام

He ﷺ is the same Allah that saved Younus عليه السلام from the darkness of the whale's belly.

He ﷺ is the same Allah who gifted Maryam عليها السلام with out of season fruits as she worshipped peacefully.

He ﷺ is the same Allah that granted Zakaria عليه السلام with the child he prayed for despite being in his old age.

He ﷺ is their Allah, and He ﷺ is our Allah too.

The difference isn't their statuses as prophets (peace be upon them all) but their level of trust and faith in the almighty Allah. That in itself is a lesson for us to learn from, to truly understand the power of viewing the world through the correct lens.

The very lens which **focuses** on what is truly in your **control** over what is not.

The lens that only **interprets** in a way that emphasises the greatness, the power, the immense mercy, and the divine wisdom of Allah ﷺ.

The lens that will constantly **scan for blessings** amidst trials and gifts during difficulties.

In this book, we will see some of the challenges Rasool Allah ﷺ experienced, alongside other great prophets and leaders, and how they conquered them through the lens that Allah ﷺ gifted them with; to inspire, teach and model for us the correct way of dealing with our difficulties without allowing them to destroy us and leave us defeated in the game of life.

Take a deep breath, send peace and blessings upon our beloved prophet's soul, and make a firm intention that you will complete any task that is given to you so that you can truly begin your journey of taking the **lead**, becoming **empowered**, and living your life in a way that serves **you** the best.

I pray that you find the peace you are looking for through this book, and that you feel your heart and soul connect more and more with Allah سبحانه وتعالى and Rasool Allah ﷺ, and our great prophets with each word your read.

I pray that you learn how to use your lenses from your first read and build up enough strength and drive to change your life forever Insha'Allah.

The Hidden Power

Allah created us with a power no other of His creations has, a power through which goals are achieved and dreams are turned into reality. A power through which legends are created and stories are told repeatedly.

A power through which Islam was born and raised. A power through which the world continues to be inspired by great individuals who passed centuries ago. A power that has been buried so deeply within us that many spend their lives not knowing they are so much more than they believed they were, that their potential was greater than they ever imagined, and their power was deeper than they ever comprehended.

It is out of the monumental wisdom of Allah ﷻ that this unsurpassed power was purposely demonstrated through the first four words that were affirmed during the first-ever remarkable incident that took place in the early days of Islam as Jibril عليه السلام made his first interaction with Rasool Allah ﷺ commanding him to read. Rasool Allah ﷺ replies in shock, confirming that he is, indeed, not a reader.

This dialogue highlights the importance of reading, especially at that time when reading was one of the main sources of knowledge. This is exactly when Rasool Allah's ﷺ hidden power began to excel as he not only learnt beyond what any average human could learn but also worked hard enough for this exceptional knowledge to be inherited by those after him.

Rasool Allah ﷺ broke the stereotypes and freed himself of the limits the people around him would set because he knew that he had power over the voices that would tell him he was not good enough and that this mission was impractical, especially since he could not read nor write.

He ﷺ knew that he had power over his emotions and every other obstacle that came his way. He ﷺ knew that our Lord would never burden a soul with more than it can bear. He knew this because he used the power he was gifted with, the very power that you too, have **always** had from the very start.

Dig for it, find it within you and use it to become unstoppable. Create the experiences you deserve, simply because Allah loves you, and did not create you with the power for any reason other than for you to utilise.

The power is yours, discover it, own it, and use it

After darkness comes the light

We recognise Rasool Allah ﷺ as our prophet, our leader, and the greatest role model. We may also perceive him as the most compassionate being to have ever walked on this planet, or as the impartial man who ensured every creature from animals and plants to humans and jinn received their full rights.

But how often do we recognise Rasool Allah ﷺ for his strength, courage, and steadfastness? Or as the inspiring man who was given the challenging duty of elevating the name of Allah and inviting every soul towards Islam, not only those around during his lifetime but ensuring that the word of truth reaches every human being till the end of time, even after he ﷺ physically leaves the world?

A mission that sounds almost impossible to complete, a substantial responsibility, extremely burdensome to carry. But he ﷺ did it. He did it with all the twists and turns, through all the thick and thin that this journey consisted of. He did it with the permission of Allah.

Despite the fear, despite the anxiety, despite the death threats, the lack of support, the bullying, the harassment the poisoning, the witchcraft… He did it despite everything that came his way because he ﷺ used the lens Allah ﷻ gifted us all with, through which he recognised that no negative emotion has enough power to consume and control any human being.

Though he undeniably felt it all. He felt what we all feel and many limits beyond that. From when Allah ﷻ ordered him to announce the truth of Islam to the people of Makkah and enlighten them that he was indeed the last prophet of Allah.

From being respected and honoured by the entire community, trusted by all with their lives, constantly being assured that anything he would say would be trusted and believed in, particularly as he stood on mount Safa to invite people to make

لَا إِلَهَ إِلاَّ اللهُ مُحَمَّدٌ رَسُولُ اللهِ

their core, their greatest value, and their guide in life, to only facing abrupt humiliation, just minutes after he was shown comforting, unconditional support by his people. Yet they belittled him, demeaned him, cursed him, and betrayed him.

May peace and blessings be upon his soul.

It was one of the hardest moments that Rasool Allah ﷺ had to experience, the moment his life changed forever. Yet he embraced his feelings, accepted them, and moved on.

He continued to preach, teach, and guide.

He continued to love, care and support.

He continued to live by his purpose and get back up every single time, undefeated and as strong as ever.

But it wasn't as easy as that. Especially when the disbelievers once noticed that the divine revelation had not been sent down from the heavens for some time. They took it as an opportunity to hurt Rasool Allah's resilience as they all knew very well that his strength was Allah.

"Your Lord has abandoned you oh Mohammed," they said, aware of this being Rasool Allah ﷺ greatest concern.

Remaining steadfast and seeing the light was not easy at this point. All he needed was an ayah to be revealed or a dream to be shown. All he needed was a sign from the almighty Allah which would soothe his aching heart and confirm that he indeed is still loved.

Day one passes, day two, day three, four, five, and six and according to some narrations it had reached up to 40 days when Jibril عليه السلام (the Angel who would deliver the messages from Allah to the prophet ﷺ) had not yet visited.

Eventually, Allah sends a beautiful, consoling gift to His beloved, a gift in a form of a surah so that we too, can receive, hold onto, take inspiration from, and live by till the very end, just like our guider ﷺ did, especially during his toughest times.

$$\text{وَالضُّحَىٰ}$$

By the morning sunlight.

Allah uses this word to describe the specific time when the sun completely rises after a long night, and the world around us is bright and comprehensible.

This ayah indicates that just as the world will face a morning despite how long the nights may be, we too will experience moments in life that will carry peace and tranquillity to our hearts. Moments that bring us relief after difficult times. Moments which remind us that, indeed, with every hardship comes ease.

$$\text{وَاللَّيْلِ إِذَا سَجَىٰ}$$

And as the darkness envelops the sky.

Because, just like moments of joy, dejection is inevitable. Hard times will arrive, and you'll feel lonely and unsupported, fearful and doubtful, but despite that, you will need to pick yourself up, stand on your two feet and face the challenges to earn better days, because these are the moments where strength truly grows; when you think you can't go on but you keep going anyway.

Just as the morning sunlight that will shine after the dominating tenebrosity of the night, the pain you feel today for every difficulty encountered will be replaced with strength, fortitude, courage, and beautiful growth tomorrow.

$$\text{مَا وَدَّعَكَ رَبُّكَ وَمَا قَلَىٰ}$$

Your Lord has not abandoned you, nor has he become hateful towards you.

One of the devil's greatest ways of trying to distance the believers from their creator is by sneaking his way into their minds to whisper emptiness and discomfort, to convince them that whatever is happening, despite how insignificant or trivial, is because Allah does not love them, and sometimes to the extent that he deceives them into believing that their sins are so inordinate that a life of misery is what they deserve.

And when that happens, remember that just as a thief will only target the wealthy, shaitan too will only focus on those rich in faith because he knows unquestionably, that if the entire world was against someone who had Allah by their side, then they have everything. Correspondingly, if the entire world was by their side but Allah was against them then they truly have nothing at all.

وَلَلْآخِرَةُ خَيْرٌ لَّكَ مِنَ الْأُولَىٰ

And the hereafter is certainly better for you than this life.

Just as the sun never shines beyond its given time and the night never settles for a longer stay. Just like the leaves on the trees today will fall tomorrow, just like the seed planted now will one day bloom. Just like good times come and go, difficult times, no matter how long they feel, will eventually pass.

In essence, everything in this temporary world, from situations to tangible items is temporary. Nothing ever lasts.

So, enjoy the auspicious moments when they come and when the unpleasant times knock on your door, let them in but as guests rather than new proprietors. When they knock, let them in without giving them the keys to control you, overtake you, dictate your behaviour and impose decisions. When they knock, let them in without giving them the power to consume you and paralyze you. When they knock, let them in as guests who will sooner or later need to leave. Let them in as guests who contribute towards making the hereafter a better place for you. When they knock, let them in because if you reject them today, they will break in tomorrow creating more destruction.

وَلَسَوْفَ يُعْطِيكَ رَبُّكَ فَتَرْضَىٰ

And surely, your Lord will give you until you are pleased.

The absence of pain without the replacement of relief is still far better than the pain itself. The gift of the complete abolishment of difficulties, without necessarily experiencing joy and pleasure is still far better than facing difficulties. But in paradise, my friend, not only will the struggles come to an end, but you will be bestowed upon endlessly until your heart is pleased, and if not for anything else then for this moment please hold on.

أَلَمْ يَجِدْكَ يَتِيمًا فَآوَى

Did he not find you as an orphan and he sheltered you?

An orphan of love we all were at some point, an orphan of support, comfort, peace, and warmth, and there's not a single time when we were abandoned, one way or another, directly or indirectly. Allah ﷻ sheltered us with His immense mercy and deep love.

The Allah who gifted us with our greatest blessings without us having to ask, who granted us life, choosing us to be believers, teaching us to walk, gifting us with instincts to protect us from pain from the moment we opened our eyes to this world, creating systems within our bodies that work 24/7 without us even realising, creating our reflex actions, blood cells that fight against diseases, and bones positioned ever so gently in our ears to help us balance. Would He the almighty, after showering you with blessings and bounties that you never asked for, not give you what you do ask for? Would He not continue to honour you, provide for you, and shower you with his love and mercy?

وَوَجَدَكَ ضَالًّا فَهَدَى

And he found you lost but he guided you.

Allah mentions in surah Ash-shouraa, verse 52:

"You did not know what the Qur'an is, or what faith is, but we made it to be such a light through which we will guide whoever we desire"

It happens to be that only 24% of the world's population are considered to be the fortunate ones who with the almighty's decision recognised Allah as the only God, and Rasool Allah ﷺ as the final messenger.

And we happen to be two individuals of the 24% whose hearts were touched by this divine light.

In most case scenarios the light was shone upon us without us specifically requesting it, and even if we were to ask for it, it is Allah and Allah alone who guides us and inspires us in asking him. As Umar bin al Khattab رضي الله عنه says:

"I'm not concerned if Allah answers my prayer, rather my concern is being guided into making that prayer because once it's made, I know without a doubt that it is heard."

This is a prime example of how we were lost but Allah guided us and how He has the ultimate power and strength to continue to do so in every way.

وَوَجَدَكَ عَائِلًا فَأَغْنَى

And he found you poor, so he gave you.

He fed you when you were hungry and always quenched your thirst. He clothed you, cured you and kept you warm. He cared for you, loved you and honoured you in a way no other of his creations are honoured.

He concealed your sins, protected you and never stopped giving. You sinned behind closed doors and He, out of His vast mercy sent oxygen to your lungs and allowed your heart to continue to beat when He had the absolute power to take your soul away and end your life in a state which will bring nothing but disgrace in the next world.

He gave and gave and gave, so much that if we were to count the blessings of the almighty, we would fail to count the smallest fraction of them, let alone all.

Yet Rasool Allah ﷺ teaches us that despite the tangible items which Allah has gifted us, true wealth lies in contentment because, whilst we are unappreciative of the little things, whilst we are unsatisfied and unpleased with what we have today, we will never value what we are given tomorrow and that is how many lose themselves in the maze of life, chasing after things that never existed when all the answers were always within them all along.

فَأَمَّا الْيَتِيمَ فَلَا تَقْهَرْ وَأَمَّا السَّائِلَ فَلَا تَنْهَر

So do not oppress the orphans, and do not repulse the beggar

By this point Allah has reminded us of all the great blessings we have been gifted with, and that there will always be those who are less fortunate than us, whether it's health wealth or wellbeing, so treat everyone with kindness and share the bounties that Allah has given you. Always lend a helping hand because as Rasool Allah ﷺ mentions in a prophetic saying: "he who supports a believer in this world will be supported by the almighty on the day of judgment" *(Bukhari and Muslim)*

وَأَمَّا بِنِعْمَةِ رَبِّكَ فَحَدِّثْ

And about your Lords bounties speak

Our creator Allah who understands us better than we understand ourselves, who knows how easy it is for us to close our eyes during dark times and unmindfully overlook what we already have by focusing on what we don't, with much love and wisdom ended this Surah by advising us to spread gratitude. To spread kindness. To spread light. Because what you give during your bright days will always make its way back to you throughout your dark nights.

And as he ﷺ mentions in the Holy Quran, "if you are thankful, he will instantly give you more."

One of the greatest ways of being thankful is utilising the gifts and blessings Allah has gifted you with in the best of ways, so the next time the darkness overpowers the light that you see in your life, remember to thank Allah for the knowledge you now have by remaining steadfast, taking inspiration from the prophet ﷺ, and not allowing any negative emotion or obstacle from stopping you from creating the life you deserve, and to live in a way where your heart is filled with gratitude, love, forgiveness, contentment, light, kindness and all things empowering while remaining mindful of Allah and navigating your way through life by trusting his divine wisdom and the portion of power he created you with.

The power of thought

Allah ﷻ out of His divine wisdom and vast mercy created the world in such a way that **nothing** has a fixed meaning.

For instance, the colour orange may not be your preferred colour, whereas someone else may experience intense joy as they find a particular product in their favourite colour, orange! Simply because the **meaning** they gave the colour orange is far deeper than the meaning others may give it.

And that is the freedom Allah ﷻ gifted us with, which happens to form a rather substantial fraction of the power we were born with. The freedom of being able to choose your meaning and interpret situations, feelings, and tangible items as you desire, is a vital tool, which if used correctly, it will help you create a better life with better experiences.

Take the example of Hannah and Sophia. Two ladies that live at the opposite ends of the world, who both happen to be anticipating for their wedding which is to begin in only a few hours. However, to their utter shock and dismay, they are both informed of an incident that took place not so long ago which involved their soon-to-be husbands and their closest friends exhibiting disloyalty and unfaithfulness.

Hannah bursts into tears of resentment and anger upon hearing the news, "why is this happening to me" she repeats in bewilderment. "My life is ruined forever, everyone I trust betrays me, maybe Allah just doesn't love me enough, maybe that's the reality and I just need to accept that I'm unworthy."

She proceeds to throw her bouquet and tosses her wedding dress as she walks out of the room, feeling the lowest she has ever felt.

Sophia, on the other hand, bows down into sujood as she sheds tears of gratitude. "Not only has Allah saved me from walking into a miserable marriage, but He also protected me from investing in someone who I thought was best for me. Allah once again has shown me that He loves me by safeguarding me and saving me for better, purer people.

As you see, the experience Hannah went through was the exact experience Sophia endured, but each of them interpreted the situation differently, hence each of them felt differently, and therefore, reacted differently, which ultimately impacts the path they are taking in life, whether they are heading towards a life full of gratitude, security, and love, or a life full of sorrow, misery, and a sense of disconnection.

Unfortunately, many of us often take a similar emotional approach as Hannah and apply it to most situations we face in life, big or small, which ultimately stops us from recognising the power we have been created with, and therefore, leads us into living a mundane life if not a wretched one.

This emotional approach is illustrated below:

SEAR

Stimulus ≫ Emotions ≫ Action ≫ Result

The **stimulus** refers to the situation that we experience, such as finding a dent in your newly purchased car, accidentally burning a cake for an order, or even being betrayed by someone close as Hannah and Sophia were.

This leads to **emotion**.

Each **stimulus** we face typically triggers certain **emotions** which cause us to react (**action**) in a certain way, producing specific **results** which are solely influenced by the **emotions** we feel and the **action** we take regarding that specific **stimulus**.

According to the example conveyed, Hannah felt betrayed, hated, unfortunate and unsafe which led her to react in a way that affected her self-esteem, her outlook on life, as well as her confidence in Allah which then left an impact on her faith. In essence, the way she felt and reacted prevented her from moving on in life and healing in a way that is healthy for her.

The diagram is illustrating the approach Hannah took, which many of us are also subconsciously led by. However, this approach misses one very important factor, and without this factor, we instantly become enslaved to our emotions, to the extent that our behaviour and our actions are controlled by how we feel.

Remember that the more you allow your feelings to control you, the deeper your power will be buried.

The correct approach:

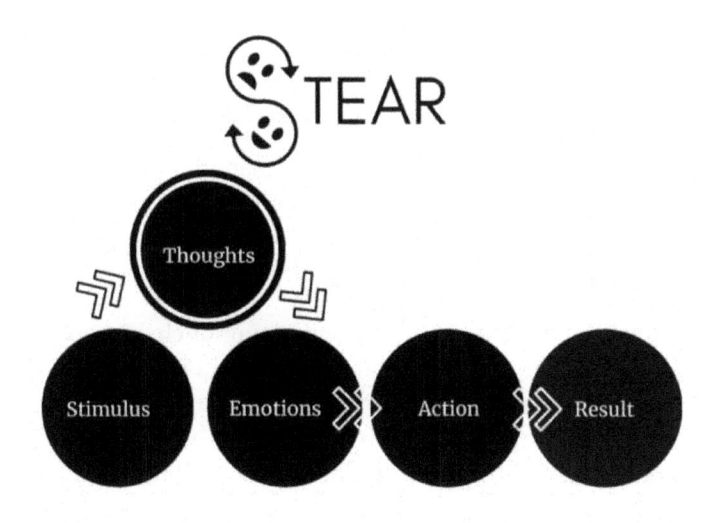

STEAR

Thoughts

Stimulus → Emotions → Action → Result

The important factor which holds the power of changing the entire game, automatically leading to better results, notable experiences and an overall greater life is the **thought** factor.

According to some psychologists, after facing the stimulus, you only have ¼ of a second to take lead and utilise the power and freedom Allah has gifted you!

Only then will you succeed in creating positive experiences and living the life you deserve, with enough strength and courage to remain undefeated, despite any challenge that comes your way.

Better thoughts= better emotions = better reactions = better results.

The opportunity you have, to **own your power** in the few seconds lies in the **thought** factor. Once the stimulus takes place, you are responsible for interpreting the stimulus in a way that serves YOU, only then will you succeed in breaking the cycle of being controlled by your emotions and gain the power you need to take lead and steer through any feeling you feel, no matter how tough or heavy.

-It was in the **thought factor** that Sophia chose to rise and see that there was truly more to life.

-It was in the **thought factor** that Rasool Allah ﷺ decided to show compassion and sympathy to the people of Taaif, despite them mistreating him ﷺ, stoning him, cussing him, and hurting him till his shoes were soaked in blood and his blessed front tooth broke.

His beloved wife Khadija رضي الله عنها and caring uncle had only recently passed. His pure heart was aching, and his soul was still grieving but spreading peace to the world and elevating the name of Allah to guide people in living a better life in this world and the next was the mission that he pursued despite the struggles he ﷺ was battling.

He ﷺ decided to travel to Taaif to achieve his objective of protecting his nation from hell fire, but they too, rejected him, belittled him, and hurt him in a way no man should ever be harmed, let alone our beloved prophet ﷺ. After being chased with stones by the entire town, injured and drenched in his blood, Rasool Allah ﷺ decided to rest his aching body under a shade of a tree he found.

His heart yearned for his beautiful wife and his great-uncle who supported him unconditionally, but they too, just as his mother, father, and grandad, had left this temporary abode.

So, he ﷺ calls out to Allah who is forever alive and shall never pass, closer to us than our jugular vein, saying:

اللَّهُمَّ إليك أشكو ضَعْفَ قوَّتي وقلةَ حيلتي

Oh Allah, to you I complain about the weakness of my strength and the scarcity of my resources

وهواني على الناس

And the humiliation I have been subjected to by the people

يا أرحَمَ الراحِمينَ، أنت رَبُّ المستضعَفينَ، وأنت ربِّي

Oh, you are the most merciful, you are the lord of the weak, and you are my lord too.

إلى مَن تَكِلُني

To whom have you entrusted me?

إلى بعيدٍ يَتجهَّمُني أو إلى عدوٍّ ملَّكْتَهُ أمري

To a distant person who receives me with hostility or to an enemy to who you have given them authority over my affairs

إن لم يكُنْ بك غضَبٌ عليَّ فلا أُبالي

If you are not angry with me then I am not concerned

غيرَ أن عافيتَك هي أوسَعُ لـي

Though your blessings are more sufficient for me

أَعوذُ بنورِ وجهِك الذي أشرَقتْ له الظُّلماتُ

I seek refuge with the glory of your light, through which all darkness is lit

وصلَح عليه أمرُ الدُّنيا والآخرةِ،

And every affair of this world and the next is set right

أن يَحِلَّ عليَّ غضَبُك أو أن يَنزلَ بي سخَطُك

That your anger will not befall on me, nor your displeasure will descend on me

لك العُتْبى حتى ترضى، ولا حولَ ولا قوَّةَ إلا بك

To you is the supplication until you are pleased, and there is no control or power except by you

---

It is then when Allah ﷻ, the all-hearing, sends his angels to pose an offer to Rasool Allah ﷺ of crushing the people of Taaif between the mountains. It's in the **thought factor** Rasool Allah ﷺ decided to reject the offer as he says to the angels "no, even if they have rejected Islam, I pray that Allah blesses their offspring to be Muslim". *(Bukhari)*

It was in the **thought factor** that Rasool Allah ﷺ utilised his power, through which Taaif today has become a town full of Muslims who not only believe in the oneness of Allah but have memorised the Quran and have become ambassadors of Islam. That is a glimpse of the power of the thought factor which we can utilize in our favour.

Now it's your turn to take heed and use the few seconds you have in your favour by including the thought factor in your approach to situations and circumstances.

Think of a time that you took the first approach "sear" and reacted in a way that caused a negative experience.

Now travel back to that moment with the knowledge you have now and the tools you have picked up and think about the **thoughts** you would focus on in that ¼ of a second. How would your *new* thoughts affect your emotions and how would your emotions affect your actions? Based on that, what results do you expect to experience?

Being mindful of every moment of your life, especially during the testing times, is not the easiest thing to do, especially if your mind is not trained to interpret situations in your favour. But it's not impossible, and if I can do it, so can you.

With firm intention and consistency, anything is possible.

I have designated a task for you to take on for 21 continuous days which you will find in part three of the book. You are asked to write about moments during your day that reminded you of Allah's love for you and you must not sleep and end your day until the task is completed in order to maximise the benefit of the task.

Do not underestimate the power of this task, start now, be consistent and watch how your outlook on life will change.

Here are a few simple examples to get you started:

-Today I saw the sunset and it reminded me of Allah's love for me as He created this beautiful world for me.

-I was about to slip but I didn't fall and that reminded me of Allah's love for me

- someone bumped my car, but I wasn't hurt and that reminded me of Allah's love for me.

-I missed the alarm so I didn't get up for work on time, but I still woke up and was gifted another day of life, another chance, and that reminded me of Allah's love for me.

Hidden gifts

By this point, we have shifted our mindset to some extent, by planting seeds of gratitude in our minds and training our thoughts to actively scan for blessings even amidst the chaos of life.

Before we begin, a very important point for you to bear in mind:

If you were to ask someone to name 3 things which they are grateful for in life, you will find that 98% of these people will only point out the very things that serve them directly.

Health, wealth, family, friends, faith, shelter, food, drink, safety, etc.

This is because we have been programmed into believing that blessings only correlate to that which we favour. The truth about this mindset is that only a fraction of our lives constitute direct and clear positive experiences, which then implies that with that thinking we are only grateful for a small segment of our lives.

What many don't realise is that the blessings we recognise actually interlocks with the very things we perceive as disappointing or dissatisfying.

For example, you may acknowledge your family as the greatest gift of all times. Yet, the loud noises, hectic gatherings, and unexpected occurrences, which you may find overwhelming and stressful, would not exist if it wasn't for the family you can't imagine life without.

The variety of the food that you enjoy happily and appreciate as a huge blessing also leads to a dreadful pile of unclean dishes by the end of the day.

The traffic and rough roads you find yourself constantly complaining about would not affect you as much if it wasn't for the car you value.

The reason why many do not see beyond the surface of this aspect is that a large fraction of society has falsely believed that one must typically "enjoy" what they are grateful for when in actual fact, gratitude is more about **recognising** that what you are dealing with right now, one way or another, serves you and contributes towards something of value in your life, whether that's growth, understanding, wisdom, light, or love, because life always happens for you.

Let that sink in

In order to reach the stage where you are fully able to redefine the negativity in your life and turn it into your strength, you must first remove the layers of deceptions to disclose the true reality through which you will eventually see the light, find the gift and receive blessings with every passing moment of life.

However, it is noteworthy to mention that even the best of people once viewed the world through a similar lens as you. Therefore, Allah decided for them to take a trip which changed their life forever, and through which many were enlightened to see beyond the surface, which shaped their understanding of how everything that takes place in life is **always** in your favour.

This incident took place years ago when a very knowledgeable man was chosen by Allah to take a path that would increase his knowledge further and teach him lessons that would deepen his wisdom and inspire many yet to come.

This journey involved spending a fair amount of time with a great leader who had a gifted insight, far from the ordinary, through which he would teach this knowledgeable man unforgettable lessons. However, the condition was that the student was not allowed to pose a single question or judge the leader for anything he was going to do.

They start their travel by boarding a boat which they were kindly allowed on free of charge. Once they arrived at their destination, the leader began to yank a part of the boat which was a complete contradiction to what the student had expected of him as he was a significant teacher with a lofty rank and an envoy chosen by Allah. This led the student to question the leader, saying "did you tear it open so that its people drown? You have indeed committed a loathsome act". The leader gently reminds the student of his condition, and they continue their journey as they leave the boat and make their way onto the shore.

As they continue to walk, they come across a group of young boys who were playing harmoniously, the leader then takes aside a young boy and kills him. The student forgets the condition as he witnesses such a ruthless act and in utter shock and disapproval he questions the leader, asking him why he committed such a crime, but the leader only responds with "did I not warn you that you will be unable to be patient with me?".

The student apologises for forgetting his promise once again and suggests that if he questions for the third time, he will leave the leader and head back home.

So, they continue their journey as they grow wearier and wearier. They stumble upon a village which they enter, hoping to find food and a place to rest. However, the people of this village refused to host them, so the leader and the student decide to leave, and as they do so, they spot a slanted wall which was about to fall so the leader heads towards it and sets it straight. The student then suggests that if the leader had taken a remuneration for the service, they would have managed to purchase some food.

This is when the leader decided that it is time for them to part ways but before they do so, he decides to share the reasons why he had done what he had done all along.

He starts by recalling the boat incident, explaining that he only damaged it to protect its people from the oppression of the king who would steal every boat that he found in a good condition, and therefore, by damaging it the king would reject it and move away which will then allow the owners to fix it and continue with their labour, away from the king's cruelty.

And in regards to the young boy, the leader explains that he only killed him due to the understanding Allah had given him which indicated that this boy would grow up to be a non-believer, which would not only bring distress and hurt to his parents but would also influence their faith in Allah undesirably, therefore… Allah planned to end the life of this young boy with deep wisdom and compassion so that the boy could reunite with his family in Jannah, whilst blessing his parents with another obedient child and a firm believer.

In reference to the wall, the leader reveals that it was no ordinary wall, as this wall was more of a protection for a treasure that was hidden beneath it. The treasure belonged to two orphans, and Allah chose to preserve it for them until they grew up and gained the capacity to discover it and look after it independently.

The leader then ends his explanation by emphasising that every action he did was a command of Allah's and that nothing was done out of his own will. Undeniably, as this great leader was indeed a chosen man named Khidar عليه السلام who was gifted with deep comprehension and a profound insight by Allah ﷻ, and the student was prophet Mousa, may peace and blessings be upon his soul.

This beautiful story has been illustrated by Allah in surah al kahaf, the very surah that forms light of protection from sins for its readers when recited on Fridays.

This was merely a glimpse into Allah's divine wisdom, providing us with the understanding that every situation we experience will **always** consist of goodness, whether we see it or not, the goodness is inevitable.

But it is **your** decision and **your** decision alone on whether you **choose** to allow yourself to recognise the gifts that every challenge brings to you.

Because life my friend, is what you make of it, and what you make of it is **your** decision, and your decision is **influenced** by your thoughts, therefore, if you truly intend to change your mindset and lead your life in the best of ways, whilst living each day with a driving purpose and a heart full of happiness, love, contentment, and excitement, you **must** take action and start to train your mind to find the light in every dark challenge.

Take the step and complete the following task **now** because as Pablo Picasso says: "Action is the foundational key to all success".

Think of a difficult time that you went through and reflect upon what the possible gifts may be. What did life bring to you through this difficulty? What did you learn? how did it contribute to your growth? How will this lesson help you handle any challenges that are brought to you in the future?

The 3 Q's

The 3 Q's that can transform your life and completely take you out from a world of dimness, overwhelming anger, uncontrolled despair, and deep confusion to a world of contentment, composure, and liberation from the shackles you have been bound by.

The 3 Q's that Rasool Allah ﷺ responded to 1400 years ago whilst he was facing one of the greatest challenges known to Islamic history. The migration.

During this period Rasool Allah ﷺ and the companions رضي الله عنهم were made to flee from the comfort of their hometown to an unfamiliar land, which they had never seen before. They had no choice but to stand up and face this tough challenge, in order to protect their lives from the horrific plots of the disbelievers, and to provide themselves with the freedom of living in security to practice their faith, which was their source of peace and the only thing they sought form this world.

The 3 Q's that Maryam عليها السلام focused on during one of the most difficult times of her life, as she experienced the agony and struggles of labour whilst being all alone in a barren land.

The 3 Q's that Mousa عليه السلام used to help him conquer the loneliness and terror he suffered from, as he left his native land, to save himself from being slaughtered alive.

The 3 Q's that can shape **your** experience in life and help **you** overcome any challenge you face are as follows:

Q1: *Own the power of focus.*

What do I choose to focus on? What I have/what I don't have

In every given moment of your life, you will have **countless of blessings** surrounding you internally and externally, but it is **your choice** to choose what you want to focus on.

When Rasool Allah ﷺ left Makkah, he lost his residency in his very own hometown, he lost his environment of comfort and familiarity. The companions رضي الله عنهم who were with him at that time had left their homes, families, friends, wealth, and entire lives behind. But they chose to focus on what they did have, because as **always**, what we have outweighs what we don't.

They had enough camels to help them to get to their destination, they had the company of Rasool Allah ﷺ whose presence they valued more than anything, but most importantly they had Allah in their hearts and the support of each other, which helped them overcome this great challenge, increased their unity, and attracted the blessings of the almighty.

Mousa عليه السلام had no choice but to run away from Egypt to save his life. He had no support, no money, no guidance, and no clue to where he was heading. But he didn't dwell on that, rather he converted his concerns into prayers and focused on what he did have, from physical strength to time and the ability to serve Allah's people.

Maryam عليها السلام was rejected by the majority of her people, so she decided to travel far away to deliver her baby, away from the cynicism of people. She began to experience contractions, so upon a palm tree she leaned when Allah ordered her to shake a branch. She was all alone, feeling her absolute weakest, with a heart full of fear and a mind full of overwhelming thoughts. Yet, she did not focus on the lack of physical strength or the isolation she was experiencing when she received Allah's command, instead she **chose** to make a conscious effort of giving her utmost best, **knowing** that Allah does not burden a soul with more than it can bear, and from that branch fell fresh dates for her to consume, to gain the strength she needed.

Q2: *Make space, take control.*

Am I focusing more on what's in my control or what's not in my control?

Despite what happens in life, there will always be things going on that you can take control of, whilst there are many things that were not meant for you to control at all. We often times lose ourselves as we try so hard to control what we can't, which is a primary way of burying the power with which you have been endowed.

Choosing to focus on what you can control will always prompt feelings of strength, empowerment, and safety regardless of the circumstances.

Being exposed to hostility and all kinds of torture from the disbelievers of Makkah was not in the control of the Muslims. So instead of working on gaining their approval and seeking their validation, Rasool Allah ﷺ and the companions رضي الله عنهم took control of how much the disbelievers were able to harm the Muslims, by placing boundaries, limiting the chances of the disbelievers and leaving Makkah. *They focused on what they could control.*

Mousa عليه السلام could not change the perspective the people of Egypt had of him, nor could he change his status and live in peace without being sent constant death threats. But what was in his control was to start a new chapter and create a new beginning for himself. He didn't know how to start or where to go, but that didn't stop him, because he knew that it is his **responsibility** to take action and the rest Allah will take care of. *He focused on what he could control.*

Allah decided for Maryam عليها السلام to carry a baby in her womb, which, as a result led to the people of her area rejecting her and belittling her but what they perceived of her was not in her control, so she **trusted** Allah with His plans and chose to do as Allah ordered, knowing that Allah will only choose for her what's in her favour. *She focused on what she could control.*

Q3: *Past, present, or future?*
Where exactly are you?

You have the complete freedom to live in the past or travel to the future or focus on the now. Going back, however, will only bring you gloom, regrets, and sorrow, whilst grasping onto the deluding illusion of the future will only increase your doubts and concerns.

Focusing on the very NOW is what will **empower** you.

Rasool Allah ﷺ and the companions رضي الله عنهم did not attach themselves to the memories of their past lives in Makkah, hoping that things would get better whilst subjecting their lives to danger, neither did they focus on the future, worrying over the drastic change that will take place once they move. *They focused on the now.*

Mousa عليه السلام did not detain himself with the memories of the luxurious life in the palace of Firoun, neither did he constantly think of what life would be like, had he not left or what exactly would happen if he was arrested and brutalised. *He focused on the now.*

Maryam عليها السلام did not imprison herself in the past where things were different, more peaceful, and less chaotic. Neither did the thought of her future as a new mother with lack of support capture her. Nor did the concept of having to face the nation as the one who Allah chose to remain pure and chaste, untouched by a single man, yet with her very own baby in her arms, consume her. *She chose to focus on the now.*

And how will **you** use the 3Q's to change the quality of your life? Will you focus on what's in your **control** or what isn't? What **meaning** will you give to the challenges you face? How will you interpret them? Will you consider it as a punishment from Allah? Or as a reward? Do you believe that Allah is unbothered about you, or that He is loving you, caring for you and protecting you? Would you think it's the end of the world or the beginning of a beautiful new chapter? What is the **gift**, what is the **lesson**? Will you **give up** or get back up again **strong** as ever? Will you **lean** back and watch Netflix, or will you **get up**, connect with your creator, and take a positive **action**? Will you moan about how unlucky you **feel**, or will you move on, take the lead, and **restore** the **power** Allah has given **you**? Will you give it a go once or twice or will you **keep going, keep doing, keep believing, keep praying, keep working** till you get there?

The choice is **yours**.

The tools are with **you**.

Its either **now** or never, you **decide**.

Part two:

Believe in your power

Your existence is far more powerful than you comprehend

When you think to yourself "what's the point", remember that Allah created you with a purpose, you were born to be better. Never doubt yourself or underestimate your ability of reaching where you intend.

You are unique and perfect just the way Allah made you, with hidden treasures buried within you, which you are yet to discover. So don't waste your valuable time and energy on what doesn't serve you or contribute towards your growth, because you have a profound, meaningful journey to get through and **if** you keep going, you **will** turn out to be the best version of yourself.

You have a purpose that you are created to fulfil. You have a designated path that will guide you to your destination. You have it within you to be everything you want to be and more. You have the qualifications. You have the ability. You have the tools and most importantly, you have the power.

The First Step

When you find yourself far from the place you want to be at, remember that you don't need to see the entire path to take the first step because the first step was never meant to be perfect. Give yourself permission to feel the doubt, to feel the fear, to feel the despondency, and take that first step anyway.

And if you feel uneasy, know that it's because we've been programmed into thinking that we need to have it all figured out and planned before we can start. But the truth is, no perfect journey is ever planned from start to finish. The good ones always take us through the unexpected twists and turns to lead us to where we need to go, and sometimes, they take longer than we think, but they will always teach us lessons we could have never prepared for, lessons that will shape us in becoming the best version of ourselves, lessons that remind us of Allah's deep love and great power.

So, when you find yourself far from the place you want to be at, just take the first step, and don't worry about what lies ahead of you, because you **will** find your way insha'Allah.

Nothing is too much for Him

There's no promise too hard for Allah to fulfill.

There's no prayer too huge for Allah to answer.

There's no problem too difficult for Allah to solve.

There's no disease too severe for Allah to cure.

There's no heart too broken for Allah to mend.

There's no sin too heavy for Allah to forgive.

There's no relationship that Allah can't restore.

There's no past that Allah can't redeem.

There's no mountain Allah can't move.

There's no enemy Allah can't defeat.

When challenges arise

As we navigate ourselves through life, there will be times we feel lost and confused, and when that happens, don't be so hard on yourself and allow yourself to fall into the deception of believing that you haven't achieved anything at all.

It is through Allah's divine wisdom and incomparable creativity that challenges and setbacks are inevitable because, truthfully, life would be dull if you had no more room to grow, or new things to learn, or reasons to keep going and get back up again every time you fall.

And remember, at the end of the day, every experience will get you to where you are supposed to be. Every loss, every heartbreak, every mistake is designed to serve you in a way that you need.

Trust the plans of Allah and believe in the power He has given you, be patient, be brave, be sincere and kind and you will eventually figure it all out, and everything will make perfect sense.

Through the bad

Allah structured this temporary world in such a way that everything in it is temporary…

Even the times you feel your mind is overwhelmed and suffocated. Or the times you feel like you can't find a way to appreciate all the amazing things that you have in life. Even the most difficult moments you endure, none of it will last. It may not feel like it right now, but these feelings **will** fade, maybe not today, maybe not tomorrow, but they **will** eventually, and you will smile again, you **will** feel like you again, you **will** experience joy and feel full of life.

Because nothing is ongoing in this provisional world, and that is a huge blessing, because through this concept you are reminded to see the bigger picture and appreciate the truly incredible parts of your days and the great people in your life because that too won't last forever.

Through this, you are reminded to be present and be in the moment.

Through this, you are reminded to always be grateful and confident that you'll get through any obstacle.

Through this, you are reminded that no matter what anyone says, you are so much stronger than what you think you are right now.

Acknowledge how you've got through every tough day in your life right up until now, and this is not any different. You'll get through this too, and you'll come out stronger, wiser, and grow into the best version of yourself.

Don't stop shining, my friend

When darkness prevails, remember that the light you can't seem to find is right within you, just as the moon doesn't see how bright it shines,

And that light, my friend, is so much more powerful than you can comprehend. Please keep sharing all the kindness and love your heart bears, without fear, even when the weight of the world feels too heavy.

Don't underestimate yourself, because I promise you there are many people out there who rely on the beauty you create and the kindness you spread. You never know who needs to be touched by a heart like yours, a smile like yours and company like yours, now more than ever.

Don't stop praying

Never limit your prayers because you think you are sinful or undeserving. Prayer was never designed for those who perceive themselves as faultless, we pray not because of who we are, we pray because of who Allah is, and because His mercy, compassion, and love for His people will always be unconditional. We pray because we have faith that His power is unmatched, and because He simply can.

So, no matter how broken you are, He can fix every part of you and put it back together. The one who created you knows exactly how to re-build you into someone better than you were, despite how impossible you think it is.

Trust Allah's plans and you will witness miracles.

Focus on the journey, not the destination

Sometimes things won't work out, and no matter how hard you try, it doesn't seem to make a difference. You feel that regardless of how high up you climb, you still seem far away from the top. And that's okay because it was never really about the view from the top anyway. It was about the beautiful person who you became on the climb up. And that is why you climb in the first place. Enjoy every moment of life, and so even if you don't reach the top, it wouldn't bother you anyway because the journey itself was worthwhile, and the fact that you summed up all your courage and strength to try, is worth more than any view you could witness from the top of any mountain.

Believe me, it all works out in the end

It's easy to get carried away with overthinking, to the point where you perhaps forget that you were never supposed to have an answer to everything in life in the first place.

You were never expected to have an answer to every feeling you feel or every situation you face. Because that, my friend, is not how life works.

Allah ﷺ structured our life in a way where we can only truly figure it all out by living. By messing up, by missing an opportunity, by seeking advice and not taking it. We learn what's important and what isn't and it's all through experience.

So, go easy on yourself, because if Allah and His ﷺ supreme Court can forgive you then why would you set for yourself a court higher than the court of the king of all kings?

And yes, sometimes we make huge mistakes that we regret, or lose ourselves completely, not knowing what to do, but it all works out in the end.

You have Allah by your side, closer to you than your jugular vein. Always trust His ﷺ plan for you, believe in the power He's gifted you and know that everything **will** work out exactly the way it is supposed to be.

It always does.

You are more than what they think of you as

You may catch yourself defining your worth based on the amount validation you receive from others. When that happens, remember that no one has enough power or control over you to dictate your worth to you, unless you allow them.

Only when you learn to fully appreciate yourself for the person Allah created you as, will you instantly stop seeing yourself through the eyes of people that don't value you.

You'll learn to stand up for yourself, you'll know that deep down, you're better than the way they make you feel about yourself, and not from an egotistical perspective but simply in acknowledgment of the honour Allah created you with as He ﷺ mentions:

وَلَقَدْ كَرَّمْنَا بَنِىٓ ءَادَمَ

And we have honored the children of Adam

You'll find more strength in that simple fact than you ever will with them, and once you find that strength you will truly feel liberated.

The best is yet to come

No matter how dark things are right now, know that brighter days are waiting ahead of you. Know that things will get better, situations will change, and you will see how the world is working in your favour. You will find new strength and discover the light that you didn't know you had within you. You will grow and rise out of these times.

And if you are walking through a wonderful chapter of your life right now, know that the best is still yet to come. Keep dreaming of growing and rising higher. Take the steps. Lead the way and don't stop because you, my friend, have more potential than you can grasp. You are incredible, amazing, and capable of anything once you put your mind to it.

So don't stop going because you have mountains to climb, and bigger dreams to turn into reality.

No matter where you are right now, always believing that the best is still yet to come.

Part three:

The key

Always remember D&E *is* the key.
D= Duaa.
E= Efforts.

The key to solving every problem you may face.

The key to every door that will lead you to your desired destination.

The key to fully unlocking your potential is D&E.

Constant duaas and a sufficient amount of effort hand in hand, and nothing is impossible!

It's the most powerful weapon you have, so be sure to use it.

The following are a few authentic prayers taught by the prophet ﷺ.

When in any difficulty recite:

اللَّهُمَّ رَحْمَتَكَ أَرْجُو فَلَا تَكِلْنِي إِلَى نَفْسِي طَرْفَةَ عَيْنٍ وَأَصْلِحْ شَأْنِي كُلَّهُ لَا إِلَهَ إِلَّا أَنْتَ

O Allah, I hope for Your mercy, do not leave me, for even the duration of an eye blink and improve my situation, there's no God but you. *(Abu Dawood)*

لَا حَوْلَ وَلَا قُوَّةَ إِلَّا بِاللَّهِ

There is no might or power, or strength expect by Allah

It has been stated in hadeeth that this prayer is the medicine for 99 ailments, the least of which is depression. *(Baihaqi in Dawatul Kubra)*

$$\text{أَسْتَغْفِرُ اللهَ}$$

Abdullah bin Abbas رضي الله عنه narrates that Prophet Mohammad ﷺ stated that if a person constantly makes "istighfaar", then Allah removes every difficulty, frees him from every sorrow and makes a means for him to receive sustenance from places that he never thought of. *(Ahmad)*

Upon witnessing a difficulty or a sin:

$$\text{الْحَمْدُ لِلَّهِ الَّذِي عَافَانِي مِمَّا ابْتَلَاكَ بِهِ وَفَضَّلَنِي عَلَى كَثِيرٍ مِمَّنْ خَلَقَ تَفْضِيلاً}$$

All praise belongs to Allah who has saved me from such a condition which is afflicted on you and favored me over many creations. *(Tirmidhi)*

The virtues of this duaa are that the reciter will be saved from the difficulties he has seen.

Upon having a nightmare, recite:

$$\text{أَعُوذُ بِكَلِمَاتِ اللهِ التَّامَّةِ مِنْ غَضَبِهِ وَعِقَابِهِ وَشَرِّ عِبَادِهِ وَمِنْ هَمَزَاتِ الشَّيَاطِينِ وَأَنْ يَحْضُرُونَ}$$

With the total words of Allah, I seek protection from His wrath, from His punishment and from His servant's evil and from the whispers of Satan and I seek protection from them coming to me. *(Tirmidhi)*

When fearing the enemy recite:

$$\text{اللَّهُمَّ إِنَّا نَجْعَلُكَ فِي نُحُورِهِمْ وَنَعُوذُ بِكَ مِنْ شُرُورِهِمْ}$$

"O Allah, we make you the turner of their (enemies) hearts and seek refuge in You from their evils".

When the enemy surrounds recite:

$$\text{اللَّهُمَّ اسْتُرْ عَوْرَاتِنَا وَآمِنْ رَوْعَاتِنَا}$$

O Allah, save our honor and remove the fear and keep us safe *(Ahmad)*

When tired of life

One should never pray for death instead pray this:

اللَّهُمَّ أَحْيِنِي مَا كَانَتِ الْحَيَاةُ خَيْرٌ لِي وَتَوَفَّنِي إِذَا كَانَتِ الْوَفَاةُ خَيْرَاً لِي

O Allah keep me alive as long as life is good for me, and when death is better for me take my soul away *(Nasai)*

When fever or pain increases

بِسْمِ اللهِ الْكَبِيرِ أَعُوذُ بِاللهِ الْعَظِيمِ مِنْ شَرِّ كُلِّ عَرَقٍ نَعَّارٍ وَمِنْ شَرِّ حَرِّ النَّارِ

I seek relief taking Allah's great blessed name from all the evils of pulling (pulsating) nerves and from the evils of the hot fire. *(Tirmidhi)*

Note: It is prohibited to speak ill of fever. When Umm Sahabia رضي الله عنها spoke ill of fever the Prophet Mohammad ﷺ said, "do not insult fever for it removes the sins of man like the furnace removes the rust from the iron".

When consoling someone:

إِنَّ لِلَّهِ مَا أَخَذَ وَلَهُ مَا أَعْطَى وَكُلٌّ عِنْدَهُ بِأَجَلٍ مُسَمَّى فَلْتَصْبِرْ وَلْتَحْتَسِبْ

Indeed, Allah has taken what belongs to Him and He has given us what belongs to Him. He has specified a time for everyone. Have patience and hope for reward. *(Bukhari)*

For any calamity

When any calamity comes, even if pricked by a thorn recite:

إِنَّا لِلَّهِ وَإِنَّا إِلَيْهِ رَاجِعُونَ اللَّهُمَّ أَجِرْنِي فِي مُصِيبَتِي وَاخْلُفْ لِي خَيْرَاً مِنْهَا

Indeed, we are from Allah and to Him is our return. O Allah, grant reward in my calamity and grant in its place a good substitute. (Muslim)

If there is pain on the body

Place the right hand on the pain, recite "Bismillah" thrice and the following duaa seven times:

أَعُوذُ بِاللَّهِ وَقُدْرَتِهِ مِنْ شَرِّ مَا أَجِدُ وَأُحَاذِرُ

I seek refuge in the Being and Power of Allah from the effects of which I am in and from that which I fear. *(Muslim)*

Duaa to pay off debts recite:

اللَّهُمَّ اكْفِنِي بِحَلَالِكَ عَنْ حَرَامِكَ وَأَغْنِنِي بِفَضْلِكَ عَمَّنْ سِوَاكَ

O Allah, save me from haraam and make the halaal sufficient and by your favour make me independent. *(Tirmidhi)*

When a companion once expressed a shortfall in his wealth to Ali رضي الله عنه responded with a duaa that Rasool Allah ﷺ taught saying: "Shall I not show you what Prophet Mohammad ﷺ taught me, even if there is a debt equal to that of a huge mountain then Allah will pay it". Ali رضي الله عنه then recited the above duaa.

When something is lost recite:

اللَّهُمَّ رَادَّ الضَّالَّةِ وَهَادِي الضَّالَّةِ أَنْتَ تَهْدِي مِنَ الضَّلَالَةِ ارْدُدْ عَلَيَّ ضَالَّتِي بِقُدْرَتِكَ وَسُلْطَانِكَ فَإِنَّهَا مِنْ عَطَائِكَ وَفَضْلِكَ

O Allah, the One who returns the lost, by Your power and awe return for me that which I have lost, for surely I have received it as Your gift and favour. *(Tabrani)*

When one's heart is filled with emotion recite:

الْحَمْدُ لِلَّهِ عَلَى كُلِّ حَالٍ

Allah is deserving of praise under all circumstances. *(Ibn Maja)*

When looking in the mirror recite:

اللَّهُمَّ أَنْتَ حَسَّنْتَ خَلْقِي فَحَسِّنْ خُلُقِي

O Allah, just as You have made my external features beautiful, make my character beautiful as well. *(Ahmad)*

When one sees a Muslim laughing recite:

أَضْحَكَ اللَّهُ سِنَّكَ

Allah keep you laughing *(Bukhari, Muslim)*

Gems from the Quran

You say: I'm a failure

Allah says: The Believers are successful

(Surah Al-Mu'minoon: 1)

You say: It's too difficult

Allah says: With every difficulty there is ease

(Surah Inshiraah: 6)

You say: I feel helpless

Allah says: It's upon Us to help the believers

(Surah Ar-Rum: 47)

You say: I feel alone

Allah says: No doubt I'm with you

(Surah Taha: 46)

You say: I'm too sinful

Allah says: He loves those who repent

(Surah Al-Baqarah: 222)

You say: I don't have much.

Allah says: If you are thankful, I'll give you more

(Surah ibraheem: 07)

You say: will it be worth it

Allah says: For those who believe and do righteous deeds is a generous provision (Jannah)

(Surah Al-Hajj: 50)

You say: I'm overburdened

Allah says: Allah will not burden a soul with more than it can bear

(Surah Al-Baqarah: 286)

You say: I am lost

Allah says: And He found you lost so He guided you

(Surah Ad-Duhaa: 7)

You say: I'm unattractive

Allah says: We've certainly created man in the best make and appearance

(Surah At-Teen: 4)

You say: I feel unacknowledged

Allah says: Your efforts and striving will be rewarded appreciated

(Surah Insaan: 22)

You say: I feel little.

Allah says: We have indeed honoured the children of Adam

(Surah Al-Israa: 70)

You say: Shytaan's plot is too powerful

Allah says: Shaytaan's plot is indeed weak

(Surah An-Nisaa: 76)

You say: Victory is far away...

Allah says: The victory of Allah is indeed close

(Surah Al-Baqarah: 214)

Virtues of sending peace and blessings upon the prophet

There are many virtues for the one who sends peace and blessings to our prophet ﷺ soul, regularly with affection and respect, some of which are:

1. Following the command of Allah.
2. Conformity with Allah sending blessing upon him.
3. Conformity with the angels sending blessings.
4. Receive 10 blessings from Allah.
5. Ten levels are raised for the reciter.
6. Ten good deeds are written for the servant.
7. Ten sins are erased from the servant.
8. Duaa is accepted if preceded with Salaah upon the Prophet ﷺ.
9. Intercession of the Prophet ﷺ.
10. A means for forgiveness of sins.
11. Allah will suffice the reciter.
12. Closeness to the Prophet ﷺ on the Day of Judgement.
13. Reward of charity.
14. A means for the fulfilment of your needs.
15. Allah and His angels send blessings upon the servant.
16. A means of cleansing and purification.
17. Glad tidings of Paradise before death.
18. Protection from the terrors of the Day of Judgement.
19. The Prophet ﷺ responds to him.
20. A means for the servant to remember what he has forgotten.

21. A means of blessings on the gathering and lack of regret on the Day of Judgement.

22. A means to repel poverty.

23. It repels the description of being a miser.

24. Protection from the Prophet's ﷺ curse.

25. Leads to the path towards Paradise.

26. A protection from the stench of a gathering where Allah and His Prophet ﷺ are not mentioned.

27. It completes speech, after Allah's praise.

28. Abundance of light on the Siraat.

29. Protection from hardness of the heart.

30. Allah bestows favourable praise upon the servant.

31. A source of blessings for the servant himself.

32. A means of receiving Allah's mercy.

33. A means to continuously love the Prophet ﷺ.

34. A means of the Prophet continuously loving the servant.

35. A means of guidance and a 'living' heart.

36. The reciter's name is presented to the Prophet ﷺ.

37. The servant's feet will be firm on the Siraat.

38. The servant fulfils a small portion of the Prophet's ﷺ right.

39. Comprises gratitude to Allah.

40. It is a duaa.

[Adapted from Jalā' al-Afhām by Ibn al-Qayyim (raḥimahullāh

Part four:

Use your power

"If you want to live a life you've never lived, you have to do things you've never done"

-Jen Sincero

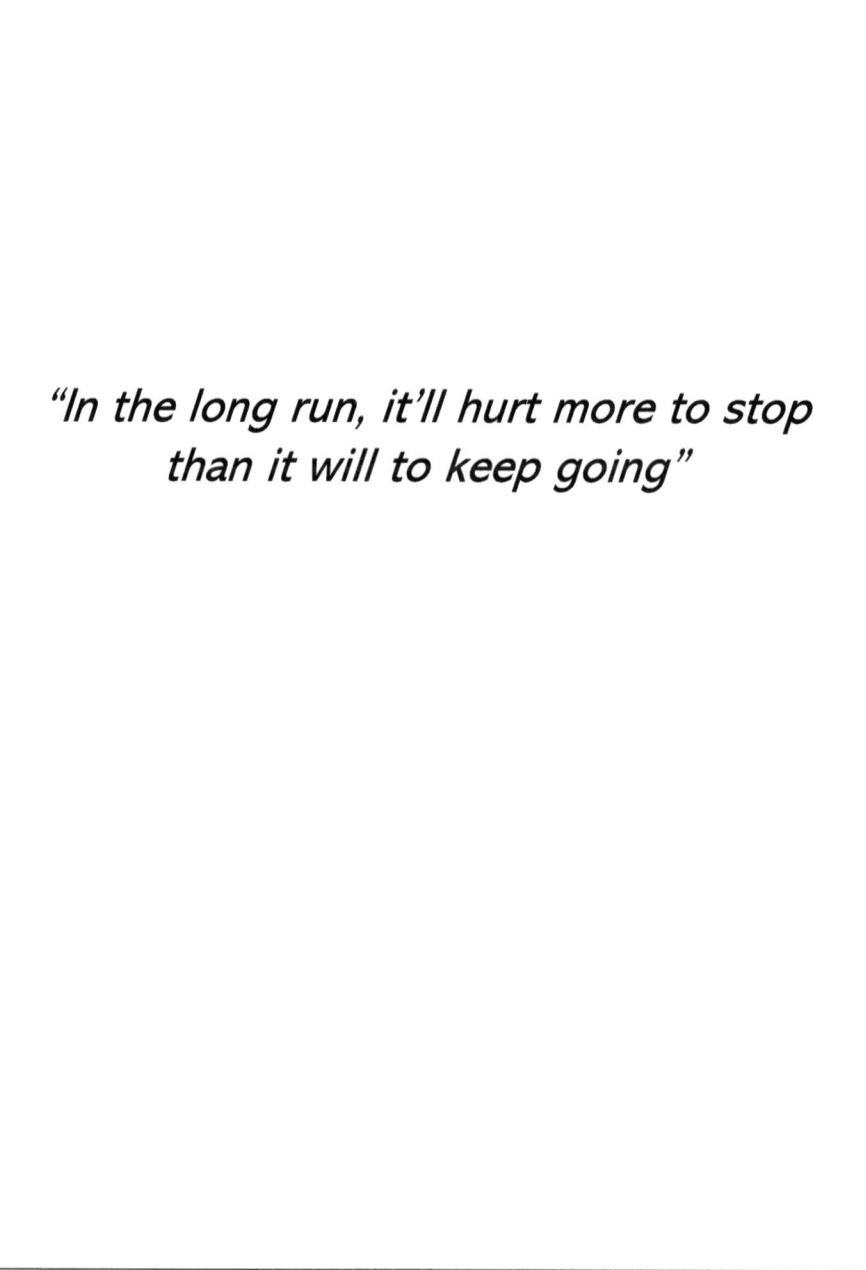

"In the long run, it'll hurt more to stop than it will to keep going"

Will it be easy?

-Nope.

Worth it?

-Absolutely!

Day 1: *Bismillah*

Morning tasks:

Things I am grateful for today:

Things I will do to make this day great:

Things I will do to be the best version of myself:

How will I connect with my creator today?

How will I follow the prophet ﷺ 's footsteps?

What do I have, and what is in my control that I will choose to focus on today?

_____
_____
_____
_____

What is the meaning of my life today?

_____
_____
_____
_____

Evening tasks:

Moments that proved Allah's love for me today:

_____
_____
_____
_____

Moments that reminded me of Allah's power:

_____
_____
_____
_____

Positive characteristics that I adopted today:

_____
_____
_____
_____

Day two: Keep going!

Morning tasks:

Things I am grateful for today:

Things I will do to make this day great:

Things I will do to be the best version of myself:

How will I connect with my creator today?

How will I follow the prophet ﷺ 's footsteps?

What do I have, and what is in my control that I will choose to focus on today?

_____
_____
_____
_____

What is the meaning of my life today?

_____
_____
_____
_____

Evening tasks:

Moments that proved Allah's love for me today:

_____
_____
_____

Moments that reminded me of Allah's power:

_____
_____
_____
_____

Positive characteristics that I adopted today:

_____
_____
_____
_____

Day three: Go, go, go!

Morning tasks:

Things I am grateful for today:

Things I will do to make this day great:

Things I will do to be the best version of myself:

How will I connect with my creator today?

How will I follow the prophet ﷺ 's footsteps?

What do I have, and what is in my control that I will choose to focus on today?

_____
_____
_____
_____

What is the meaning of my life today?

_____
_____
_____
_____

Evening tasks:

Moments that proved Allah's love for me today:

_____
_____
_____
_____

Moments that reminded me of Allah's power:

_____
_____
_____
_____

Positive characteristics that I adopted today:

_____
_____
_____
_____

Day four: Consistency is key!

Morning tasks:

Things I am grateful for today:

Things I will do to make this day great:

Things I will do to be the best version of myself:

How will I connect with my creator today?

How will I follow the prophet ﷺ 's footsteps?

What do I have, and what is in my control that I will choose to focus on today?

What is the meaning of my life today?

Evening tasks:

Moments that proved Allah's love for me today:

Moments that reminded me of Allah's power:

Positive characteristics that I adopted today:

Day 5: Enthusiasm is common, endurance is rare!

Morning tasks:

Things I am grateful for today:

Things I will do to make this day great:

Things I will do to be the best version of myself:

How will I connect with my creator today?

How will I follow the prophet ﷺ 's footsteps?

What do I have, and what is in my control that I will choose to focus on today?

_____
_____
_____
_____

What is the meaning of my life today?

_____
_____
_____
_____

Evening tasks:

Moments that proved Allah's love for me today:

_____
_____
_____
_____

Moments that reminded me of Allah's power:

_____
_____
_____
_____

Positive characteristics that I adopted today:

_____
_____
_____
_____

Day 6: It's on you to get you where you need to be!

Morning tasks:

Things I am grateful for today:

Things I will do to make this day great:

Things I will do to be the best version of myself:

How will I connect with my creator today?

How will I follow the prophet ﷺ 's footsteps?

What do I have, and what is in my control that I will choose to focus on today?

_____
_____
_____
_____

What is the meaning of my life today?

_____
_____
_____
_____

Evening tasks:

Moments that proved Allah's love for me today:

_____
_____
_____
_____

Moments that reminded me of Allah's power:

_____
_____
_____
_____

Positive characteristics that I adopted today:

_____
_____
_____
_____

Day 7: ONE THIRD DONE!

Morning tasks:

Things I am grateful for today:

Things I will do to make this day great:

Things I will do to be the best version of myself:

How will I connect with my creator today?

How will I follow the prophet ﷺ 's footsteps?

What do I have, and what is in my control that I will choose to focus on today?

What is the meaning of my life today?

Evening tasks:

Moments that proved Allah's love for me today:

Moments that reminded me of Allah's power:

Positive characteristics that I adopted today:

Day 8: Don't stop now!

Morning tasks:

Things I am grateful for today:
_____
_____
_____
_____

Things I will do to make this day great:
_____
_____
_____
_____

Things I will do to be the best version of myself:
_____
_____
_____
_____

How will I connect with my creator today?
_____
_____
_____
_____

How will I follow the prophet ﷺ 's footsteps?
_____
_____
_____
_____

What do I have, and what is in my control that I will choose to focus on today?

What is the meaning of my life today?

Evening tasks:

Moments that proved Allah's love for me today:

Moments that reminded me of Allah's power:

Positive characteristics that I adopted today:

Day 9: Keep going, you've got this!

Morning tasks:

Things I am grateful for today:
```
------------------------------------------------
------------------------------------------------
------------------------------------------------
------------------------------------------------
```

Things I will do to make this day great:
```
------------------------------------------------
------------------------------------------------
------------------------------------------------
------------------------------------------------
```

Things I will do to be the best version of myself:
```
------------------------------------------------
------------------------------------------------
------------------------------------------------
------------------------------------------------
```

How will I connect with my creator today?
```
------------------------------------------------
------------------------------------------------
------------------------------------------------
------------------------------------------------
```

How will I follow the prophet ﷺ 's footsteps?
```
------------------------------------------------
------------------------------------------------
------------------------------------------------
------------------------------------------------
```

What do I have, and what is in my control that I will choose to focus on today?

_____
_____
_____
_____

What is the meaning of my life today?

_____
_____
_____
_____

Evening tasks:

Moments that proved Allah's love for me today:

_____
_____
_____
_____

Moments that reminded me of Allah's power:

_____
_____
_____
_____

Positive characteristics that I adopted today:

_____
_____
_____
_____

Day 10: Push yourself to do the things you think you can't!

Morning tasks:

Things I am grateful for today:

Things I will do to make this day great:

Things I will do to be the best version of myself:

How will I connect with my creator today?

How will I follow the prophet ﷺ 's footsteps?

What do I have, and what is in my control that I will choose to focus on today?

What is the meaning of my life today?

Evening tasks:

Moments that proved Allah's love for me today:

Moments that reminded me of Allah's power:

Positive characteristics that I adopted today:

Day 11: Halfway there, well done!

Morning tasks:

Things I am grateful for today:
_____
_____
_____
_____

Things I will do to make this day great:
_____
_____
_____
_____

Things I will do to be the best version of myself:
_____
_____
_____
_____

How will I connect with my creator today?
_____
_____
_____
_____

How will I follow the prophet ﷺ 's footsteps?
_____
_____
_____
_____

What do I have, and what is in my control that I will choose to focus on today?

_____
_____
_____
_____

What is the meaning of my life today?

_____
_____
_____
_____

Evening tasks:

Moments that proved Allah's love for me today:

_____
_____
_____
_____

Moments that reminded me of Allah's power:

_____
_____
_____
_____

Positive characteristics that I adopted today:

_____
_____
_____
_____

Day 12: Keep going, all this hard work will be worth it in the end!

Morning tasks:

Things I am grateful for today:

Things I will do to make this day great:

Things I will do to be the best version of myself:

How will I connect with my creator today?

How will I follow the prophet ﷺ's footsteps?

What do I have, and what is in my control that I will choose to focus on today?

_____
_____
_____
_____

What is the meaning of my life today?

_____
_____
_____
_____

Evening tasks:

Moments that proved Allah's love for me today:

_____
_____
_____
_____

Moments that reminded me of Allah's power:

_____
_____
_____
_____

Positive characteristics that I adopted today:

_____
_____
_____
_____

Day 13: You already have what it takes.

Morning tasks:

Things I am grateful for today:
_____
_____
_____
_____

Things I will do to make this day great:
_____
_____
_____
_____

Things I will do to be the best version of myself:
_____
_____
_____
_____

How will I connect with my creator today?
_____
_____
_____
_____

How will I follow the prophet ﷺ 's footsteps?
_____
_____
_____
_____

What do I have, and what is in my control that I will choose to focus on today?

_____
_____
_____
_____

What is the meaning of my life today?

_____
_____
_____
_____

Evening tasks:

Moments that proved Allah's love for me today:

_____
_____
_____
_____

Moments that reminded me of Allah's power:

_____
_____
_____
_____

Positive characteristics that I adopted today:

_____
_____
_____
_____

Day 14: it's a slow process but quitting wont speed things up!

Morning tasks:

Things I am grateful for today:
_____
_____
_____
_____

Things I will do to make this day great:
_____
_____
_____
_____

Things I will do to be the best version of myself:
_____
_____
_____
_____

How will I connect with my creator today?
_____
_____
_____
_____

How will I follow the prophet ﷺ 's footsteps?
_____
_____
_____
_____

What do I have, and what is in my control that I will choose to focus on today?

What is the meaning of my life today?

Evening tasks:

Moments that proved Allah's love for me today:

Moments that reminded me of Allah's power:

Positive characteristics that I adopted today:

Day 15: BE STRONGER THAN YOUR EXCUSES!

Morning tasks:

Things I am grateful for today:

Things I will do to make this day great:

Things I will do to be the best version of myself:

How will I connect with my creator today?

How will I follow the prophet ﷺ 's footsteps?

What do I have, and what is in my control that I will choose to focus on today?

What is the meaning of my life today?

Evening tasks:

Moments that proved Allah's love for me today:

Moments that reminded me of Allah's power:

Positive characteristics that I adopted today:

Day 16: Almost there!

Morning tasks:

Things I am grateful for today:

Things I will do to make this day great:

Things I will do to be the best version of myself:

How will I connect with my creator today?

How will I follow the prophet ﷺ 's footsteps?

What do I have, and what is in my control that I will choose to focus on today?

What is the meaning of my life today?

Evening tasks:

Moments that proved Allah's love for me today:

Moments that reminded me of Allah's power:

Positive characteristics that I adopted today:

Day 17: So so so close!

Morning tasks:

Things I am grateful for today:

Things I will do to make this day great:

Things I will do to be the best version of myself:

How will I connect with my creator today?

How will I follow the prophet ﷺ 's footsteps?

What do I have, and what is in my control that I will choose to focus on today?

_____
_____
_____
_____

What is the meaning of my life today?

_____
_____
_____
_____

Evening tasks:

Moments that proved Allah's love for me today:

_____
_____
_____
_____

Moments that reminded me of Allah's power:

_____
_____
_____
_____

Positive characteristics that I adopted today:

_____
_____
_____
_____

Day 18: There's a past version of you that is so proud of how far you've come

Morning tasks:

Things I am grateful for today:

Things I will do to make this day great:

Things I will do to be the best version of myself:

How will I connect with my creator today?

How will I follow the prophet ﷺ 's footsteps?

What do I have, and what is in my control that I will choose to focus on today?

What is the meaning of my life today?

Evening tasks:

Moments that proved Allah's love for me today:

Moments that reminded me of Allah's power:

Positive characteristics that I adopted today:

Day 19: 3 days left!

Morning tasks:

Things I am grateful for today:
_____
_____
_____
_____

Things I will do to make this day great:
_____
_____
_____
_____

Things I will do to be the best version of myself:
_____
_____
_____
_____

How will I connect with my creator today?
_____
_____
_____
_____

How will I follow the prophet ﷺ 's footsteps?
_____
_____
_____
_____

What do I have, and what is in my control that I will choose to focus on today?

_____
_____
_____
_____

What is the meaning of my life today?

_____
_____
_____
_____

Evening tasks:

Moments that proved Allah's love for me today:

_____
_____
_____
_____

Moments that reminded me of Allah's power:

_____
_____
_____
_____

Positive characteristics that I adopted today:

_____
_____
_____
_____

Day 20: Two days left!

Morning tasks:

Things I am grateful for today:
_____
_____
_____
_____

Things I will do to make this day great:
_____
_____
_____
_____

Things I will do to be the best version of myself:
_____
_____
_____
_____

How will I connect with my creator today?
_____
_____
_____
_____

How will I follow the prophet ﷺ 's footsteps?
_____
_____
_____
_____

What do I have, and what is in my control that I will choose to focus on today?

_____
_____
_____
_____

What is the meaning of my life today?

_____
_____
_____
_____

Evening tasks:

Moments that proved Allah's love for me today:

_____
_____
_____
_____

Moments that reminded me of Allah's power:

_____
_____
_____
_____

Positive characteristics that I adopted today:

_____
_____
_____
_____

Day 21: YOU MADE IT!

Morning tasks:

Things I am grateful for today:
_____
_____
_____
_____

Things I will do to make this day great:
_____
_____
_____
_____

Things I will do to be the best version of myself:
_____
_____
_____
_____

How will I connect with my creator today?
_____
_____
_____
_____

How will I follow the prophet ﷺ 's footsteps?
_____
_____
_____
_____

What do I have, and what is in my control that I will choose to focus on today?

_____
_____
_____
_____

What is the meaning of my life today?

_____
_____
_____
_____

Evening tasks:

Moments that proved Allah's love for me today:

_____
_____
_____
_____

Moments that reminded me of Allah's power:

_____
_____
_____
_____

Positive characteristics that I adopted today:

_____
_____
_____
_____

CONGRATULATIONS!

A huge well done to you for putting up and making it to the end!

I am so proud of you and cannot wait to hear all about your achievements, success stories, positive changes, and the new life you have created for yourself.

Send me an email on Maariadeem@gmail.com

or drop a DM on Instagram @Maaria.deem

Feedback on the book is always welcomed on:

www.maariadeem.com

May Allah increase the love, light, warmth, and wisdom within you.

May He continue to guide you to using your power and keep you close to Him until you meet Him in the next world.

Sending you prayers, Maaria Deem.

www.ingramcontent.com/pod-product-compliance
Ingram Content Group UK Ltd.
Pitfield, Milton Keynes, MK11 3LW, UK
UKHW020628200225
4677UKWH00020B/386